The Instruments of Art

JOHN F. DEANE was born on Achill Island in 1943. He founded Poetry Ireland – the National Poetry Society – and *The Poetry Ireland Review* in 1979. He is the author of many collections of poetry and some fiction. His poetry includes *Christ, with Urban Fox* (Dedalus Press, 1997), a collection translated into several languages, *Toccata and Fugue: New and Selected Poems* (Carcanet, 2000) and *Manhandling the Deity* (Carcanet, 2003). His poetry has been published in French, Bulgarian, Romanian, Italian and Swedish translations. John F. Deane's prose works include two novels, *In the Name of the Wolf* (Blackstaff Press, 1999), published in German translation in 2001, *Undertow* (Blackstaff Press, 2002), and a collection of short stories, *The Coffin Master* (Blackstaff Press, 2000). In 1996 John F. Deane was elected Secretary-General of the European Academy of Poetry. The recipient of the O'Shaughnessy Award for Irish Poetry in 1998, and the Grand International Prize for Poetry from Romania in 2000, in 2001 John F. Deane was given the prestigious Marten Toonder Award for Literature. His poems in Italian, translated by Roberto Cogo, won the 2002 Premio Internazionale di Poesia Città di Marineo for the best foreign poetry of the year. John F. Deane is a member of Aosdána.

Also by John F. Deane from Carcanet

Toccata and Fugue: New and Selected Poems
Manhandling the Deity

JOHN F. DEANE

The Instruments of Art

CARCANET

Acknowledgements

Water-Stone, Hamline Literary Review (USA), *Asheville Poetry Review* (USA), *The Southern California Review* (USA), *La Traductière* (Paris), *The SHOp*, *Poetry Ireland Review*, *Irish Writers Against War* (O'Brien Press), *Irish Pages*, *Agenda*, *New Welsh Review*, *Southword*, RTÉ 'Sunday Miscellany' and Lyric FM 'The Quiet Quarter'.

'The Meadows of Asphodel' was a prize-winner in the Cardiff International Poetry Competition. Several of the poems have been presented in the 'Waxwing Poems from the House of Icarus' series. The title poem 'The Instruments of Art' won the 2004 Ted McNulty award, was translated into Italian by Chiara De Luca and published in *Poesia* (Crocetti Editore). The poem 'Riverdown' appeared in *Something Beginning with P*, ed. Seamus Cashman (O'Brien Press). The group of poems collected here under the title 'The Old Yellow House' was published in a limited edition with six screeen-prints by John Behan, by Red Fox Press, www.redfoxpress.com, and given the title 'The Old Grey House'.

The author wishes to thank An Chomhairle Ealaíon, The Arts Council Ireland, for a residency grant that enabled him to finish this collection, and Villa Waldberta, Feldafing, Germany, for the three months spent in that residence as guest of the city of Munich.

First published in Great Britain in 2005 by
Carcanet Press Limited
Alliance House
Cross Street
Manchester M2 7AQ

A CIP catalogue record for this book is available from the British Library
ISBN 1 85754 786 1

The publisher acknowledges financial assistance from Arts Council England

Typeset by XL Publishing Services, Tiverton
Printed and bound in England by SRP Ltd, Exeter

Contents

for Ursula

I The Instruments of Art

Canvas

I had been reasoning with myself, had grown
angry, resolving nothing; thought of this charnel earth,
its sodden meadows, its daub, heard how it cries
come! put your hand here and feel my wounds!

Times like this, fretful, I long to glide
from the rim of the turning wheel, down the long spoke
to the centre of peace. I remember how father's
quick-lifted hand would cross a blessing on his life

before a journey and how, coming out of church,
his fingers sprinkled a tiny mist of thanks
from the stone stoup; the same big hand
that soothed me, mornings, into wakefulness;

and how I was hurt when he found that centre
where he is at rest. My own warm fingers
touched his frosted forehead and I wished him
every possible blessing on that journey. A small

message of rain has riddled across the rooftop
and evening sunlight touched the floor; I looked up
and saw how the legs of the swift tuck tightly in;
I watched through the skylight where clouds

puckered and shoved, assuming spaces, shapes;
sometimes a rook came black against the darkening sky
and once a heron passed, like one of those heaving crates
from an old war; above me then the world

was a Botticelli masterpiece, allowing
mystery its scope till I flung wide the skylight,
inhaling all God's bitterness and dalliance
and the curious slow turning of the stars.

Heirs to a Different Century

I

It was May; in Sunday best we walked around
The church in slow procession, while bells were rung
To cheer our pilgrimage over familiar ground;
Words like *hosanna* chimed a homely tongue
And when they spoke of lilies of the field
I thought of 'flaggers' and of meadowsweet
Where we rose snipe or teased out golden eels;
And our hearts brimmed, like water, like wheat.
It was a child's estate, bordered by the white
Unsullied mayflowers; out over the sea
Gannets dived across immaculate light,
Streams beyond the gate flushed pure, flowed free;
You, my God, were my living God, and I
Your son, unprodigal, unselfless, shy.

II

May; the old man stepped off the evening train
as if the platform moved; *is this*, he said,
Zion? and laughed, and stumbled, while I heard
Lindisfarne, Iona, Rome. I knew
he had never climbed the cloud-enshrouded
pilgrim-mountain of his mind, or crossed,
still faithful, the spirit-plains. There is, he said,
no purpose, nor can we live without some purposes.
I dreamed the ships he had been labouring on
shifting on featureless oceans, I saw him
drifting blindly through hot engine-rooms
with his oil-rags, his sweat-weakened, blackened
face, his sumped, dispirited soul, and held his hand –
hero, and tumbler – leading him towards home.

III

It is May; on the world's jagged edge
where sea-reach and pounding have cracked
the rocks and gouged out crevices, I walk
with caution, mindful of the rigour,
the haul of life's demanding; in from the sea
the black hag comes, urging its rag-feathered body
low over the water, intent, as if there could be
direction, until a sudden squall shifts it
erratically seawards. Familiar. Strange.
Sometimes I stand exulting, breathless
before the mystery; in clean water
off the pier, sea weeds sway with the sway
of the ocean; and down the coast a boulder
fox poses on stones like a ballroom dancer

IV

while the wind's fine and artful fingers
riffle lines of gold along his fur. Today
the lifeboat has gone out from Achill
in a high-spring gale; somewhere on Blacksod Bay
fishermen hold to their craft and prayers;
what fine white flesh is a man's, could be
swallowed down God's gullet
with an excellent white wine. And see!
This is a day I would cry magnificat!
Save that at my back and in my soul
the human rage continues and turd-brown
poison seeps downriver towards the sea. Soon
the storm will ease, leaving a high tide
brimming full, like darkness, or like light.

V

No red gate here to be shut
against marauding cattle, now
only black-sheened wrought-iron bars
against blackguards blundering
like badgers across the night,
smashing car-windows, trampling
well-ordered picture-gardens;
the soup-grey sky is underlit
by a saccharin-orange glow
with few stars visible; one
fast-moving light is a police
helicopter scouring man's
estate, while individual disorders
are being quieted again in sleep.

Late October Evening

We sat and watched the darkness close
– like a slow galleon under black sail
nearing; and grew conscious again of those
of our loved dead who might come, pale

in their murmuring group, up the long road
towards us. Thrush and blackbird hurled
valiant songs against the gloom as though
this was the first dying of the world.

You and I drew closer still
in the fire's glow, grateful this far
for love and friendship, while the low hill
melded with the dark and a perfect star

swung on its shoulder. When I turned back,
near sleep, to hold you, I could pray
our dead content again under black
sails, the tide brimming, then falling away.

Riverdown

... Comes dribbling out of high peatlands,
innocent places, shriven; out of
marshy hollows, silent humplands where
mist-clouds shift and darken; from under

heather hemp-roots and moss-whorls,
the secret tracks of foxes and the
rending-places of the hooded crow;
gathering, down towards the white-washed

gable-ends of outhouses, grows
a stream, with eels like molten butter and
backs the colour of peat, their bellies
a softened gold, they shiver under low banks

by half-buried stones where drips of rain
plop-plapppp off the couch grass ...

... Come in now under this bridge, and crouch,
child-small, the water gravelling shallowly;
touch the flake and moisture of the masonry,
inhabit for a while a tiny

nowhere, be lonely, stone, be fluid;
sometimes a car will pass above you,
the world will shudder and unnatural
ripples rake the water; only attend,

fall to absence, be unseeing, all
listening; somewhere close a wren jitters,
perhaps a skald from the upper fields
offers its harsh-pitched groan; you could be

child forever, a washed-down tree-root,
perfect, useless, desire stilled ...

... Stood, often, on bridges, watching down
and dropped something, twig or leaf
and ran, watched it show on the other
side – and gloated as if a victory

had been won; time it takes to run from
arch to arch, from twig to schooner, for
the child to fall to unbelief; water
runs out gold over smoother time-stones

in pools; sounds come human, the flat-lands
reached, where dullness stretches out
towards sea; in a curve the water deepens
to a pond, surface-still and dangerous,

the first dark holding; in the distance
the monastery bell calls noon,

... angel-mystery, pause, to touch
earth, and turn again, as if something
has been declared; now you can drop your
home-made hook, worm impaled, the cork

focusing the louring afternoon; all
the rivers of the world flow down
into the sea and the sea won't
overflow; the trout, thumb-small,

feed on oozings from the mountain; brown
furzelands, bog-iris, rushes thriving
on marsh acres, stream fattening to river,
here and there a donkey brays or

cows plash into muddying water;
drag forward, restless, the hope always

for that one trout, throbbing and fleshfull,
that nervous kill; till dogs bark and you
climb barbed wire into someone's meadow;
sorrow now that your pilgrimage down

from high places has wearied you.
The pleasure is the travelling, see how tide
reaches here, how marshland melts to slob,
stench of decay, mud-bubbles, mullet

sluppering in the shallows, gulls
raucous by the pier's excesses, and your spring
has disappeared into sea-rot. Knowledgeable, something
achieved, gather yourself still for the endeavour,

hold onto longing for the one
centre, the life-force, home, the mystery ...

The Gift

And did you catch it then? That offered flash
of brilliance across the gloom? There by a curve
of the river, by the salleys and ash-trees, a brash
iridescence of emerald and blue –
kingfisher! Skulking you were, and sulking, astray
from sacrament and host, with your dreary
dwelling on the ego. Pathetic. Pray
grace in that sacred presentation, the high
shock of what is beautiful leading you to betray
this self-infusion for a while. And then that cry –
its piping *chee-chee-chee*, secretive by the stream's drift
and you step closer, cautiously, grace being still
easily squandered, till you have it before you: the gift!
Loveliness, and a dagger-like poised bill.

Rhododendron, Fuchsia, Thorn

for Thomas Dillon Redshaw

Here wretch creep
into the thornbush's comforting
of spine and blossom, of contorted limb;

bogland stretching like desert places,
gold-bloom and bird-feather on the whin,
blood-flakes, sun-stain;

hillock and árdán of the marsh,
grape-coloured low-slung places where the mind
flings itself about like the morning lark.

Big Tom Molloy with his big fists, became for you
the limit imposed upon beloved chaos
and bullied you back into furze bushes

where you were stung and punctured into tears; this
the sorrow begun in childhood,
the necessary acquiescence in the fall,

the Jesus-child grown wise before his time
and Elijah, weary, who stretched his body out under a furze bush
and wished his life were dust.

*

Stood, healed but abashed, on the sand-rutted lane
between fuchsias; noon; the gate-lodge blue, forget-me-not,
the bike strewn where he had fallen, and all pride
swashed out in tears and the tut-tut-tut of the nurse;

the perfect rowan-berries of blood on knee and elbow,
on his palm a stippling of gravel-dust, the blood
berries plumping; trespasser, punished already,
discovered, scolded, cured. Stood then, incapable,

the world's too rapid wheeling stunning him foolish.
She came, daughter, rounding the driveway curve, something
gossamer in her fending, something steel-blue in the way
her prettiness suggested perfectibility; and

laughed at him, and said his name, and plucked
one fuchsia flower to squeeze a nectar drop
down onto his wrist; oh then his wounded soldier
stance, till she bent and licked the juice with her quick tongue

scorching his flesh; and laughed again and disappeared
back round the driveway curve, leaving him
more abashed, more healed, sensing the possibilities
of trust, the tactile interventions of the beautiful.

*

At dusk I climbed a fence into the wood
and all the treetops
lifted in a racket-harmony of starlings;

surge of guilt again, its shivering excitement.

Shush-shifted among the treetrunks
across the ancient littering of leaves and branches
and took the pebble-path towards outhouses;

an alien god, I was told, and the devil's pincers;

big cattle came, lurching towards me
like an audience, quizzical and eager to be pleased;
the stranger's house, the Major, protestant

and threatening out of its height, its gloom;

I peered through a high window into other worlds,
salon, great mirrors, antlers on the high wall,
plaques of old gallantry and privilege

till I stood islanded beyond islands, and islanded

in confirmation of the softer icons of my living,
the vulnerable pathos of my own place
and the long consolation of our fireside prayers.

*

Here then is God's finger, twig, arthritic,
and this His spittle, sap-flow and rising,
these the leaves and blood-spray blossoms
singing the green songs of the birds,
these His strophes and heart-beats, and you,
and all, are blown about in sensuous
wind-movements, the motions of an unrehearsed
jerky ballet, seeking to find the perfect
dying-place, the angle. So are your days
and you accept them, and if time hangs heavy
time too is the thrust and energy, the violent
spilling and breaking, and all of it is God's
stultifying closeness in the blood, His wearying
absences about the black roots in the clay.

By the Banks of the Dodder

The poet Yeats could have been this bird
– high and watchful; artificer;
attentive, through the image of himself,
to the river's flow;

poet at prayer, such
concentration and advertence, such slow
stepping across familiar ground
with the deadliest intent.

On the alder branches, strips of plastic,
of rag detritus
as round the holy wells and wishing-places
where miracles certainly happened;

creaking old bird, with shattered wing
dragging, in miserere,
towards the underbrush, where God has died
for the white heron.

The Visitors

These are the drawky days, and we exist
like Paul the hermit, our ribs
as the thorn bush, and all the world
despicable in its ordinariness;

I am a wayfarer and a pilgrim on the earth,
each day I ask: put a new song in my mouth
that I may speak with the tongues of men
and of angels. Three waxwings

perched on the winter rowan, exotic birds,
sleek and crested, flashes of crimson and gold
across these dun days. An arctic chill
had touched the gardens like an unseen angel,

the branches of the tree showed filigrees of frost
and every insignificant sound
crackled across the air with instant messages;
when I turned the birds had disappeared

but I was smitten by the wonder of the rowan,
this visitation of the marvellous
upon the ordinary, the world about me
singing for a moment a soft hosanna.

The Rowan Tree

There is a sense of this as imposition,
the greening, blossoming, and the curt showing
of scarlet berries. Till nudity returns

and stillness, the dark flesh gleaming under rain
and the solitary robin visible again in its singing
of the grace to be found in endurance.

The Meadows of Asphodel

The gate leans crookedly and blue binding-twine
clamps it against strays. Over peat acres
bog-cotton sways like a chorus of souls arrayed

for paradise, prepared to utter into praise.
In this humped meadow the individual graves
are clothed in dogrose and montbretia, clumps

of soiled-white lilies and the tut-tut-tutting
wheatears. Neglect, I say, and you say
repose, how the dead have abandoned us, become

seeds curled in darkness, their only task to wait
the nourishment and ripening; here it is the living
are blown about by the winds. The stones

with their weathering, their burthen of names
and aspirations, face, you say, all in the same
direction, and I say, East, waiting

for that disturbance, the grincing of the gate
when we will all stir out of repose, and lift, prepared
for counting, like pale down shivering before the breeze.

Adagio Molto

I see them, Father, Son and feminine Spirit,
through the nothingness of space and absence,
in a passionate passacaglia, happy to be getting
nowhere; creating, in repose,
harmony, time, the rhythm of the seasons.

And I see the girl, young still in the soul's
heavenward journey, gravity and grace in her decorum,
standing obedient to the forces of clay and cloud that make
Vivaldi: *Gloria*
in excelsis Deo, fingers of the left hand

alert with wisdom, the right dictatorial, commanding
the winds and waves of the prayer. She, also,
passionate and at work, like this window–cleaner –
questions, too, of gravity and grace –
who hangs by threads at the twenty-seventh floor,

sheening glass to a metaphor of clouds
in a high, unblemished sky. Sounds from the world
are rumour merely, and it will not be easy –
in terra pax – to come down
and walk once more among the citizens.

Three Rivers

I hold to you in the warm darkness beyond midnight,
your presence gracing my days with purpose, my nights
with permanence. Sometimes I reach for you and there is

no more than the down-current of abandonment, dread –
in your absence – wrapping me about. Once I sat
by a great river, willow leaves, green–gold, idled

on the water; I was attentive for a while
to the swirlings and inwash after the lumbering
down-passage of a ship, and grew aware once more

of the longings in me for perishable, lovely things, knowing
that you were with me, even in your absence. Came that
ravaging, down-wheeling flight of the shell-duck, their

wheedling and gathering, how they splash-skidded to a halt
on the current's rush, till I recalled that day we sat
at another water's edge, sharing the gossip of our individual

pasts, you resting your head on my shoulder, till we knew
that day was an everlasting day, that the mystery of what stays
forever is the mystery of the glory of perishable things.

The Instruments of Art

Edvard Munch

We move in draughty, barn-like spaces, swallows
busy round the beams, like images. There is room
for larger canvases to be displayed, there are storing-places
for our weaker efforts; hold

to warm clothing, to surreptitious nips of spirits
hidden behind the instruments of art. It is all, ultimately,
a series of bleak self-portraits, of measured-out
reasons for living. Sketches

of heaven and hell. Self-portrait with computer;
self-portrait, nude, with blanching flesh; self
as Lazarus, mid-summons, as Job, mid-scream.
There is outward

dignity, white shirt, black tie, a black hat
held before the crotch; within, the turmoil, and advanced
decay. Each work achieved and signed announcing itself
the last. The barn door slammed shut.

*

There was a pungency of remedies on the air, the house
hushed for weeks, attending. A constant focus
on the sick-room. When I went in, fingers reached for me,
like crayfish bones; saliva

hung in the cave of the mouth like a web. Later,
with sheets and eiderdown spirited away, flowers stood
fragrant in a vase in the purged room. Still life. Leaving
a recurring sensation of dread, a greyness

like a dye, darkening the page; that *Dies Irae*, a slow
fretsaw wailing of black-vested priests. It was Ireland
subservient, relishing its purgatory. Books, indexed,
locked in glass cases. Night

I could hear the muted rhythms in the dance-hall; bicycles
slack against a gable-wall; bicycle-clips, minerals, the raffle;
words hesitant, ill-used, like groping. In me the dark bloom
of fascination, an instilled withdrawal.

*

He had a long earth-rake and he drew lines
like copy-book pages on which he could write
seeds, meaning – love; and can you love, be loved, and never
say 'love', never hear 'love'?

The uncollected apples underneath the trees
moved with legged things and a chocolate-coloured rust;
if you speak out flesh and heart's desire will the naming of it
canker it? She cut hydrangeas,

placed them in a pewter bowl (allowing herself at times
to cry) close by the tabernacle door; patience in pain
mirroring creation's order. The boy, suffering puberty, sensed
in his flesh a small revulsion, and held

*

hands against his crotch in fear. Paint the skin
a secret-linen white with a smart stubble of dirt. The first
fountain-pen, the paint-box, pristine tablets of Prussian Blue,
of Burnt Sienna – words

sounding in the soul like organ-music, Celeste and Diapason –
and that brush-tip, its animated bristles; he began at once
painting the dark night of grief, as if the squirrel's tail
could empty the ocean onto sand. Life-

drawing, with naked girl, half-light of inherited faith,
colour it in, and rhyme it, blue. In the long library, stooped
over the desks, we read cosmology, the reasoning
of Aquinas; we would hold

the knowledge of the whole world within us. The dawn
chorus: *laudetur Jesus Christus*; and the smothered,
smothering answer: *in aeternum. Amen.* Loneliness
hanging about our frames, like cassocks. New

world, new day. It is hard to shake off darkness, the black
habit. The sky at sunset – fire-red, opening its mouth
to scream; questions of adulthood, exploration of the belly-flesh
of a lover. It was like

the rubbling of revered buildings, the moulding of words
into new shapes. In the cramped cab of a truck she, first time, fleshed
across his knees; the kiss, two separate, not singular,
alive. It was death already, prowling

at the dark edge of the wood, fangs bared, saliva-white.
Sometimes you fear insanity, the bridge humming to your scream
(oil, casein, pastel) but there is nobody to hear, the streaming river
only, and the streaming sky; soon

on a dark night, the woman tearing dumbly at her hair while you
gaze uselessly onto ashes. Helpless again you fear
woman: saint and whore and hapless devotee. Paint your words
deep violet, pale yellow,

the fear, *Winter in Meath, Fugue, the Apotheosis of Desire.*
The terror is not to be able to write. Naked and virginal
she embraced the skeleton and was gone. What, now,
is the colour of *God is love*

when they draw the artificial grass over the hole, the rains
hold steady, and the diggers wait impatiently under trees? Too long
disturbing presences were shadowing the page, the bleak
ego-walls, like old galvanise

round the festering; that artificial mess collapsing
down on her, releasing a small, essential spirit, secular
bone-structure, the fingers reaching out of *need*, no longer *will*.
Visceral edge of ocean,

wading things, the agitated ooze, women on the jetty
watching out to sea; at last, I, too, could look
out into the world again. The woman, dressed in blue, broke
from the group on the jetty and came

purposefully towards us, I watched through stained glass of the door,
and loved her. Mine the religion of poetry, the poetry
of religion, the worthy Academicians unwilling to realise
we don't live off neglect. Is there

a way to understand the chaos of the human heart? our
slaughters, our carelessness, our unimaginable wars?
Without a God can we win some grace? Will our canvases,
their patterns and forms, their

rhymes and rhythms, supply a modicum of worth?
The old man dragged himself up the altar steps,
beginning the old rites; the thurible clashed against its chain;
we rose, dutifully, though they

have let us down again, holding their forts
against new hordes; I had hoped the canvas would be filled
with radiant colours, but the word God became a word
of scorn, easiest to ignore. We

*

came out again, our heartache unassuaged.
The high corral of the Academy, too, is loud with gossipers,
the ego-traffickers, nothing to be expected there. Self-
portrait, with grief

and darkening sky. Soon it will be the winter studio; a small
room, enclosed; you will sit, stilled, on a wooden chair, tweed
heavy about your frame, eyes focused inwards, where there is
no past, no future; you sit alone,

your papers in an ordered disarray; images stilled, like nests
emptied; the phone beside you will not ring; nor will the light
come on; everything depends on where your eyes
focus; when

the darkness comes, drawing its black
drape across the window, there will remain
the stillness of paint, words on the page, the laid down
instruments of your art.

II The Artist

The Artist

I   Condemned to death

On the translation of power into love:
there is no intervention once it has begun;
and it has – begun. Fresh are the pastures, and above
snow-drifts, crocus-fingers reach towards sun.
I loved her then. The rafters of our church were crude
creosoted wood, and images along the wall
were rough, hand-painted, two-dimensional –
a simple progress, simply to be followed.
And here, one man translates Christ's agony :
these piercing branches, tormented sky thick-filled
with clouds: the painter's aim – transform necessity
into care. This is the Christ's long-time-willed
offering of himself to judgement, while we
are wombed in a recess of rock, old wisdom stilled.

St Joseph's, Bunnacurry, Achill Island

II   Taking the cross

You leave the small island of your hidden days
for the necessary journey. Winter geese
shift along the tideline through the city's waste,
birdwatchers huddle on the road, voluble in the ease
of Sunday afternoon, their lenses trained.
God the artist holds us always and in every way
wracked across a frame: to take the strain
of the brute earth, the cross. You will portray
the handsome Jewish face lifted in vain
towards implacable heavens, the fair cheeks flushed,
eyes pleading, all guilt transferred to the divine
absence. Here nib and ink, watercolours, brush –
first instruments for the management of flesh.
Our islandman, so young, exiled, and knowing pain.

Mungret College SJ, Limerick

27

III   The first fall

Because by your cross... the rough wood, that nude
distorted foot, flaws in the timber, saws' scream
in the forests. We see cattle slaughtered, flung onto crude
fantastic pyres; a twenty-four-hour dream-
like burning, flesh, hide and skull and our days
obscured; the human divine, between creation
and the first fall. Daffodils stand in a cut-glass vase
in a scent of chapel-of-repose; in the stations
of the spirit earth and sky play one another's part.
Is this our God? Stumbling. Is this His glory? This bright
blood-red mantle is the Christ's, this ghastly white
you give to his flesh. These, the instruments of your art:
constancy and flux in colour and in light,
the rhythms of the form, the integrity of heart.

Our Lady of Mount Carmel, Firhouse

IV   Meeting the mother

The empty church, redolent still of incense,
contains, more than the folksy alleluias,
the vastness that a fugue contains, and absence
rich as the blood-light in the distant glass;
here deep affliction speaks itself, a mother
come to plead, kneels wordless, watchful. It is she
who has made the pattern clearer, out of another
climate, a distant century, an identical humanity.
Our hurry lays them down across the road – red
fox, night-badger, rat – like pieces of old
rope or washed-out floor-clouts; how to redeem
all slaughtering into care? The artist painted
his city in a harmony of greens, in grey-cold
apocalypse, as though attendant, a waking dream.

Kimmage Manor, Dublin City

V Simon of Cyrene

We have found the source of the madness of God –
inside a walled garden, under the lassitude of trees,
in the slow ease of pebble-walk and flower-bed –
self-immolation, the lovers' walk. This
too is the generosity of God, and earth's daughters
coifed in love. After the Sunday roast, the slow
turn on the pier, the trawlers berthed: when slaughter
has been hosed from the decks, the timbers still show
veins of blood. Brush-tips in the gentlest style –
virginal white on pear-tree and plum; the small
crosses on the sisters' graves claim shares in the cross
of Christ. Can God be shamed? Can you paint God's fall
in human colours? This, then, the divine guile:
inveigling us towards madness, sharing human loss.

Poor Clare Convent, Drumshanbo

VI Veronica

A heron, inelegant and beautiful, came
flopping down over the valley, this grim place
where crocuses with their delicate purple flame
already are blowing out. Between His image and God's face
we stand, obstinate, like walls; how a man can kill
another man, how the German dead out of two
world wars lie exiled; old rock-mouths, the few
artistic wreathes, this grave suggestive skill
as if Christ's face were stone. A mountain hush, snow
lingers in scoop and quarry, a mountain breeze
across the pines, and water-music; below
the slopes are brown and ochre, dumped among the trees
are rust-coloured burnt-out cars, sketching a dearth
of purpose, Christ's face again imprinted on the earth.

German Cemetery, Glencree

VII   The second fall

Grit-welts on the palm, sweat and nausea, the fear
you count for nothing, reaching the zero of your state;
each fall will be forgiven, and each collapse create
more human bearing. God in the dust comes near
the utmost of our being. This artist, Christ. Whom
we elevate in glorious windows, in cold
vaults reaching skywards, where tablet and tomb
tell the rage of kings and the stubbornness of the old
saints. We seek the metamorphosis of stones
to prayer, of prayers to stone, the fallen people's cry
for the reaches of purity. Like the rattling of bones
hard-heeled shoes click on the slabways, candleflames try
for lightness. This, the weight of our pleas and moans
on the earth, and Christ's hands lifting us on high.

Canterbury Cathedral

VIII   Women of Jerusalem

In the distance the ocean, and the great islands;
you must stoop low here, where our God has slept
centuries in dampness; where the roof of His love, like strands
of the mothers' hair, brushes your features. Who have wept
over our progress towards dissolution. These days
the city brightens to a cherry-blossom glow,
old words resurfacing: cerulean, emerald, cerise;
it is the intersection of the worlds, God brought low
for our ascension. If walls collapse upon our children
do we not scream? Earthquakes, floods, horrors of age
and suffering in the blood of all things: the artist, again
drawing our glories down to zero, where God can pass
through our heart's fragility back into His image:
that tiny heart-house no acreage of canvas can encompass.

Gallarus Oratory, Kerry

IX   The third fall

I bind unto myself today the Three
in One, the One in three; against the body
of the earth my limbs lie wracked: can you be
closer to us than this? felled and bloodied.
The Greek has painted long and delicate
fingers and even the black knots of the cross
are veined with love. The aisles are cold, ornate
marble dulled in dust, the effigies and embossed
timbers sour and generous as that old Dean.
O Christ my soul is thirsting for you and my flesh
hungers. Unanticipated hailstones thresh
against the leaded roof while a grim, lean
sunlight flickers on the aged walls. Wild geese fly
north again; the world turns. Towards a darkening sky.

St Patrick's Cathedral, Dublin

X   The stripping

Espolio. Crowds, like tourists: it is easy to remain
anonymous, the Christ amongst us, his robe – rent
apart – an intense red; see how they strip away
power from the God, with the God's consent,
till men become a surging force. They run
urgently about, the bearded, the foolish, the good,
warriors thrusting bravely at him, while one
stoops apart, preparing nails, levelling the wood –
how to reduce divinity to quivering flesh.
In the old city, dream city, this April Friday,
processions pass, drumming for applause; buzzards in a grey
sky soar, the zero circle. Can man, the artist, start
from here, take canvas, oils, palette and brush –
make them the instruments of power, and of a loving heart?

Toledo, the Cathedral

XI The nailing

That sheep may safely graze... they are playing Bach
when I come in; baroque display, the more violent
St John, and in the chapel lateral, the Black
Madonna, of carved walnut, shaped and elegant,
powerful against Plague. Can you draw harmony
from the hammering of nails into stretched wrists?
Lambs, in the corner of a field, under rain,
infected, the truck drawn up and waiting in the lane;
primroses, elemental yellow, where God exists
as power, and daffodils drooping along the drain.
It is expedient for all that one... How effective
the instruments of men's art, and how divinity
has subjected itself to the consequences: love
hammered into the earth with deliberate cruelty.

Church of St John, Luxembourg

XII The death

Sheep's hooves skitter on the ramp, and a truck leaves
green pastures; dark eyes wide with terror can be seen
watching out from between the laths. The earth heaves
in obedience, under the murdering boots of men.
This, too, is unacceptable that one must die
in violence, for our kind. Zero point, breath-
taking canvas and riotous hill, lover high
on his masterwork of pain. Trinity of thieves and death.
Voices echo in the great naves, the flagstones lead
all to the centrepiece, El Greco: the crucifixion; clam-
orous angels gathering blood, the man-god dead
and alabaster-cold; a canvas washed in the blood of the lamb
as if, with thickening oils, the painter's skill
can transform such murdering power so the heart falls still.

Museo Nacional del Prado, Madrid

32

XIII   Taken down

The hyacinths, in groups, have come to bloom, their scent
generously disturbing; destructive things stir, too,
in gardens, in obedience. The *Pietà*, paint
tempera on panel, signed: a tiny, compact group
blent in grief; an ever richer palette here, the wood
abandoned, clouds reared like mountains, and only
the man-god, god-man, is at peace. The Lord
my Shepherd, in the valley of darkness I'll not fear.
Effete and plaster saints in the side aisles
hold rose and lily; we celebrate this day
in hyacinthine purple. Under hawthorns, in the grime
of winter, sheep lie still as discarded bales
where jackdaws perch. Little is known of him yet we may say
this was the greatest artist of all time.

Church of St Pius X, Templeogue

XIV   The tomb

In the bare-veined elms the swelling clots yield
twig-nests of the excitable, familiar daws. Now
they have dug a pit large as a playing-field
to take the carcasses; we have seen sheep and cow
dumped from the beds of trucks. Soon it will be dawn;
there will be bird-song, over an acreage of death;
we have laid our handiwork down in a womb-
like recess of rock, and sent the one who gave us breath –
the image-maker, into the dark below.
I touched her coffin, seeking release from pain;
the wood was polished, patterned and stained
while incense rose, and the choir sang; such instruments.
In April once, Toledo – 'dominico greco'
received the sacraments, and died. Now everything depends…

St Joseph's, Bunnacurry, Achill Island

III The Old Yellow House

House at the Crossroads

The front door had a brass knocker
with frosted, ice-coloured glass on either side;
when I heard Beethoven's Fifth symphony for the first time
I remembered mother's anxious reaching for the door;

out there, beyond, there is a blueprint
of this family, but too much distance
across the blank expanse of space
and too much interference from manmade

and un-created things; old house, all
dead, dispersed, and those present have no sense
of the true occupants of this house.
I have come again

to listen to the old chants, to knock on that front door
like one who has taken every road away
and has returned, burdened; only the beloved dead
will be there to answer, to throw open

the familiar door. If you let reason
fall, like a blue antique tureen, the scent
of mystery will pervade the house;
for now a storm plays about the walls,

the wind, in a high soprano voice, intones
Vivaldi: *nulla in mundo pax...* the rain
against the windows is Tallis's
miserere nostri and down the chimneys

an alto saxophone moans *Kyrie*;
I am embraced again in protective blankets,
in the small light on the Pilot wireless,
with the bolted door between me and the world.

The Study

Over the deal table a flower-patterned oil-cloth;
the boy
has his Bible history open before him; its pictures

of deserts, and of stylised heroes of God's militias;
he is chewing on a pencil-end
as if hunger for knowledge frustrates him and he spits

small splinters out onto the stone-flagged floor;
outside
hydrangeas are in bloom, their sky-blue flowers

big as willow-pattern plates; on the kitchen wall
a picture of Jesus, stylised,
fingers long as tapers, ringlets honey-brown, and eyes

lifted querulously towards the ceiling;
a red, eternal light
flickers weakly below the picture;

but the saddened eyes have lowered, and peer
down on the restless
stooped-over boy, in anger or in mute and trenchant

pleading;
and only a summer bee
distraught against the window, makes any sound.

Carpenter

Grandfather's grave
lies amongst rank disorder; a high stone cross
holds the history of the world
carved in pastel-coloured lichens; the graveyard path

hides in weeds and grasses; St Joseph lilies flaunt
white and unkempt surplices; it is creation's
original chaos of delight –
where the old man lies, at peace, like God

before he shook himself out of lethargy
and spoke. *In the beginning...* But at times,
on quiet summer nights, the old man takes a turn
about the yard, tidying away

the empty beer and cider cans, the condoms,
and works a while on polishing his soul
against the final word that will draw
everything back to stillness. The way he used to hone

his workshop tools, because the old man's God
was a carpenter God
whose every word sent some new craftwork out
into the universe

to spin, and swell, and reproduce. You can hear
grandfather make his way back down,
sounds like woodshavings being swept,
like a workshop door being shut.

The Monastery

I was sent down for milk. Evenings. Knocked, scared,
on the scullery door. A yellow light
from the chapel windows; figures within

unshaped and cowled, in some intimate dance
with their dark Christ. A sour silence
smelling of man, of curds, and of wet stone floors.

I turned, and the yellow light
sent shadows shifting through the orchard trees,
their bitter, arthritic limbs, boned

fingers, armpits, the writhing
creatures of the drowned ark. Up on the road
moonlight sometimes, the thump of my own feet

on Tarmac, all the irrational rational dread
thudding in my soul till the distant house
beckoned to me, home, and the music that light makes

tuned its strings for me so I could run,
certain again of familial warmth, of the oil lamp
softening the eyes of Jesus on the kitchen wall.

Sheltering Places

The water, old-gold and bog-brown, leaches
down from the peat hillsides and the deaths
of ferns; his makeshift passages across the lake
are on tossed-together planks and canvases
with the winds that roister down from the hills
whispering heather-fragrances to him, telling
of the secret pleasure of loneliness, while the reeds
gossip in sheltered places – till the boy's body,
masterful and taut, tensed with the mystery,
tells how he knows already that there will be
no answers, and knows too (the tip of his skiff
nudging the bank where fox has dumped
feather-trash and gristle) that he will spend always
on the waters of such lakes, drifting for answers.

The Mysteries

When the old man died, grandmother –
reaching back, as he did, to the nineteenth century –
took charge of the mysteries, the joyful,
sorrowful, and the glorious; she had retired
into blacks and greys, for out of darkness, she would say,
we come, and into darkness
we must go. Each night we knelt,
the rules of recitation fixed; after the last
'glory' and 'amen', the silences; elbows hard
against the hard seat of the chair, knees
sore against the flagged floor, we floated
into our privacies. Nanna.
I watched her face, the old flesh, talced and spotted,
closed eyes lifted as if she would see beyond
the darkness of our fall, to a bright
redemptive country where those she had borne and loved
walked again, unhurt, the Christ
walking, too, and I saw tears
ease themselves onto her cheeks till her whispering
was the whole structure of the mysteries,
the words and the Word, flesh
distilled to grief and love, and all this gravity
a straining towards the invisible.

The Ship

She was sitting in the striped deck-chair, the dog
dog-dreaming at her feet; the summer garden,
a noon-time listless as a tide before the turn;
I was floating stick-ships on the drain, imagining

gardens greater than this, and more fabulous;
if I let them go they would float past almost
endless obstacles, into the chaos
of the sea; when mother

shivered, and sat up, startled suddenly
and said: somebody
has stepped across my grave. Now,
I remembered it, where I was sheening the black

marble headstone and at once –
wind in the puzzle-trees and rain spittling –
our world of clay was a fabulous boat
floating out on an ocean of darkness.

The Siege

She was held by Christ, but not the Christ
of light and lightness, by Him
who has convinced the world of sin, of the lust
of flesh, and of hauteur. She had come

to this cell-like bedroom, its dimness, a plain
dressing-table with its small, scented
illusions of holding age at bay. She sat
on the side of the bed, to repeat

her Legion of Mary prayers, her lips
sounding as of silk papers rustling. And I
could not forgive her that she had glimpsed
one side of the face of God, judgement, high

established laws of unmalleable being, and I call
out to her now in useless grief, who have lost
one whose eyes turned on me with care, whose walled
fortress I had breached, whose faithfulness, and whose Christ.

The Old Yellow House

I am ghost presence still
haunting ghosts in the crossroads house;
blind-man's-buff in the hallway –
a shadow, reaching to touch

shadows, father's ghost hands teasing.
Upstairs, end of the landing, the boy
prayed, words cupped like moths in his hands
and they would not fly, as if

our natural aspirations scorch
against Christ's flame. I would follow
a figure in the sky, shoulder-bones
like wings, lifting off the island into light.

I remember father's fingers, how they brought
shadow-butterflies to life along the wall; father,
mother, all the beloved dead – it has become
questions of gravity and grace, a holding

to Christ begging from the shadows, as I hold
to lake and house and living ghosts,
attempting to release the words like prayers
that they rise towards the Christ-shadow, the light.

IV According to John

You

I am sea-born, and sea-inclined; islanded
on this earth, dragged each-which-way, and tidal;

senses shifting as the sands shift, my soul
flotsam. Prisoned in time, and you, love,

are eternity, you are the current in my depths,
my promised shore. And when I part from you,

taking my words to dry, sophisticated places, I am
tugged towards you, sweet desperation, this underwater storm.

One for Sorrow

Potato-peels and chicken-bones, egg-shells, fish-heads and -tails,
dumped over the wall into the pine-grove;
in the fragrance of escallonia, this was locus
for day-dreaming, for the boy's
lurid imaginings and absences.

Now I have come back, like a thief, to stand
in the heavy greatcoat of adulthood, to listen to the rain
drip through thinning foliage,

and to touch, again, the un-life that passed this way
before me, that survived a while where I have been,
on sea-nourishment, rehearsing
limb-movements, imbibing knowledge
of the gravity without.

*

If we begin in ignorance, not sin, if we acquire
error only as we grow, becoming
centres of our own desiring, with webs extending
out from us – then he, still-born, was born perfected.

The bleak-stone hospital, chickweed growing in the walls,
and mother, in the grim ward moaning, the sweat
and tearing, her two hands
holding to the bed-bars; and then

the wet head showing, its small plastering of hair, all
orifices on the world shut tight
in full refusal. Was there pain? A baptism?

Would they have given him my name?
The numberless dead massed about, and waiting.

*

I stand, where he never stood, hold-
ing his space and hesitation
between not-flesh and flesh,
know how his birth-song
began as requiem, false notes played
on flawed instruments in the ongoing cacophony.

*

Mother comes to the brightly painted
back door of the house,
stands in a patch of sunlight and stares
straight into my eyes, until I turn
away, confused, though that

was half a century ago and she has found
her lost, unmentioned son again;

she and sadness, growing old together, something
that swelled between her and light, between her and me,
and I speak, *John, John,*
into dark spaces between the trees;

a solitary magpie
watches, his high-gloss
tail-feathers twitching, meaning
trespass,
and scolds me loudly, and lifts
away
into the trees. I scuff

the layered pine-needle-falls, reveal
a tiny vegetal riot, grub and maggot
in bloated white until tears come, and prayers, guilt
that I have climbed these trees, my hands
graced with resin, and known the joy
of breeze and sky, the breath of necessary being, and I ask

*

forgiveness for existing,
rain in my hair, misting onto my glasses,
that I forgive myself and her, she me,
I him, for being there and not there –

and someone, something, passes, in a white gown, silently
through the day-dusk, the tree-gloom, the decay.

Lady

Light through the lemon tree, late summer
green, sheen on the bruised fruit, a sweet
bitterness, like love songs, like longing. Take

care of her, he said, his lips frothed
with blood and spittle, but she has been water
between my fingers and never would accept

the gravity of sorrow. Now she is old bones –
yet how can wearied flesh seem quick
and beautiful? – she is the river hurrying

to re-enter sea – the old tidal pressure
restraining her, the deepening. Arthritic
fingers bicker with the sheet as if, where she lies,

she would become flame, lifting; harsh
breathing, her limbs so feather-fine with pain
that if I turn my back on her a moment

she will have disappeared, like light, like grace.

The Jacaranda Tree

Noon. Heat shimmering over the white-washed walls
of the back yards, the tree

swollen with light. The morning chores
set by, I was sitting, dulled. Attending. Only the tick-

tack stitching of cicadas, the creak
of contracting timbers. Under astonishing clarity

I laboured to be zero, to be a force like the wisdom-force
in the tree's sap,

obedient.
There was a threshold of light

that the light crossed, a physical
absence, like a body of light, a query,

intrusive, thrusting; not a word uttered, not one
word, but I filled with the being of God and

consented. When I recovered senses my young girl's breasts
pouted with pleasure, and my belly, hollow yet with longing, felt

patient, taut. And I knew there is not any person
counts for anything, nor any angel.

The Divine Office

Born, out of the torn
zero of a woman, into innocence, and sin: the divine
plan – that God should abdicate out of all quiet, split
being into might, and love, setting self up
for crucifixion – is not a human
lunacy. I remember the man who stood,

barefoot, on market day, out on the road,
to open his fly and piss onto the world, all
grin and knuckle-bone and thin as a wild briar: God's
blood-blackened finger-nails
scraping about in a man's brain. That
was earlier. I remember

a high, dark building, mockery of rooks
in the sycamores outside;
beyond scuffed, brown doors were nests
of the greatest sorrow, lives
confined within grim spaces; I remember
her lunate eyes, and how they died, how her trembling hand

shaped and undid
unseen beings in the air. When she died
did her soul walk out unfettered
on sparkling waters above the sky-line, her being
alert again with wisdom? That, too,
was earlier. I watched

out a small window; the yellow zero of the moon
half-lit a neat quadrangle, a stone calvary
casting its crazed shadows;
my being was sour with discontent
as if I had sucked on the pith of lemon-fruit,
pretending sanctity. On my pillow

a small brass crucifix, to invest my dreams
with the leer of death,
as if the human office, too,
were to unstitch the ego wholly. We had sung
Compline, had shuffled sleepily
towards the Great

Silence; the cherry-tree was virgin-still in star-light; spring
night, my young man's body
juddering; I, given life
only to renounce it, Brother
John, his black soul hanging on the door, his black
shoes in order by the bed.

I would have laid my head in rest
on the breast of Jesus, meaning *love*, meaning
abandon, to hold
always and only
loneliness in my arms, and emptiness, the mind
spinning in dizziness like a stunned wasp. Oh John, Oh Brother

John, clean-shaven and intent,
content a while in cincture, collar, stock,
but in need – and this was later – of the whelming
love of woman that would sweep away
the reasonable
into the foolishness of love.

Of Misery: The Other John

Of witness: concerning light, how it flickers
on the surface of the river the way we, too,

are nothing, not we

matter, but must decrease as body
wastes. The other John, briar-creature and disconcerting,

cactus-spirited, what is invisible in the heart
and most difficult in the will

manifest in him: vituperation, self-immolation, woe.

*

I watched him stand in the river's flow,
minnows of darkness and light

pimpling about his calves; his stillness
was all desire, would scour world and self

transparent to the sight of God; stooped
to scoop water over on himself, would be

salmon, open-mouthed, impelled upstream towards the source.

*

I feared him, who worried at his life
like a mongrel worrying a bone, the slow

death-tango his vocation, and his need.

*

Crowds came, hungry in a land of light
for news of light, his dervish hands

attempting to draw away the veils

from the face of God. Leaf-light and shadow
stippled him a moment beautiful though I would weep for him,

his argument being sin, and wilderness, and must.

Suffer the Children

Noon. Spring-time. Again that hushed and cherry-blossom
first-communion purity, the smaller birds
insistent in their mating-songs, and the word *grace*
hovering like a blue-day sea-mist everywhere.

In my dream the children, loose-limbed and clamouring, irritate
the Christ; but today they are staring out at us
from make-shift beds in make-shift wards, the children
who have been washed over and over in the Lamb's blood.

South of Jerusalem Israeli tanks
have been rumbling into Beit Jalla;
a child's pink ballet-shoe
lies in the rubbled buildings of Jenin;

I remember, on the school-room wall, a painting,
Christ's hand gently on the head of a child,
John, the apostle, bustling others away, and underneath,
the words *Suffer the little children.*

*

Upstairs, back of the cupboard, the Start-rite box,
a pair of shoes, tiny pink hearts
on the half-scuffed toes; kept,
treasured, and forgotten. But remembered

one night, an almost tropical
underwater funk and desperation, kettles, steam,
the child (named Mary, cherished)
exhausted in the labour of breathing; till,

panicked at last into where we should have been,
we raced through the city coloured death,
streetlight like tainted moonwater, the actual world
uninhabitable; a nurse

snatching the motionless body, rushing her
out of our hold, leaving
one blue-wool shoe, discarded, to be stuff
of nightmares. A tap

dripped loudly
in a porcelain sink; we waited,
understanding
whirling round and round in the sink-hole.

*

A prayer may be (how can I say this?) this
emptiness, this waiting, incomprehension, this
imponderable hanging – breathless –
on the mercy of God.

*

Out on the lip of the cliffs, with the vast Atlantic
breathing out and breathing in on the beaches and shingles below,
the small hard grass-humps of the lost
babies, those

who had chosen to die in the flooding waters
of birth, those
we could not cope with, nor understand,
nor pray for, nor pray to –

cast at once out of our ken to the world's edge.
Raise
small crosses now, small
patterns of white shore-stones, and beg

forgiveness, for our ignorance, our innocence,
there where the fulmar soar, where flotsam ends,
where the hurt seal comes flopping out of ocean
to find rest.

Master of the Feast

Together we chewed and sucked upon fresh lemons,
    tiny-stippled like human skin, our faces
        spasming with the bitterness of it, the cleansing,

tears in our eyes, the soft pith clinging – oh my
    belovèd Palestine, belovèd
        earth. We were sitting, tipsy, on the low stone wall

between lemon-grove and house, voices
    murmuring under the trees, a girl's laughter; just he,
        and I, and the night sky, and the surface of things

split wonderfully open. He was chuckling, his index finger
    picking at loose stuff between the stones. Was it
        red wine, or white? I don't remember, our lives

water, our current, hope. The ordinary
    slope of the hill, terraces under starlight, the dull
        plain of Battauf leaning towards the lake;

after the ceremonies, the feast; two days of a gentle
    roistering, the moistening of mind and limb to joyfulness.
        The hard, plum-leather skin of the pomegranate

broken, that sweet-acid and blood-bitter, sensual flesh-pulp,
    the seeds
        lingering in the teeth, lush-shock and ultimate

satisfaction. My belovèd
    Palestine. My belovèd. The mother
        in the fullness of attention, waiting. He had said

we would see the opening of the heavens and the angels of God
    descending and ascending. She called him
        out of the dance. Reluctant. I could see

the danger – if we did not know the man
    how could we cherish the divinity? It was a night
        when all the stars seemed to be

re-assembling themselves, and all this
    ascetic earth, the water-pots and firkins,
        this nowhere-place, cactus-bed and dust-yard,

and I reached my hand on the stone wall
    and touched his restless fingers, wondering. It was a night
        when the clichéd words of hope

formed song. Our lives
    are water. Oh my belovèd
        Palestine. My belovèd.

Angelus

Blind-man's buff in the hallway, a shadow reaching
for shadows: the boy
prayed, in the upstairs room, his body hooped
in concentration, the words
cupped in his hands like moths, and they would not fly,

as if our natural aspirations scorch
against Christ's flame. Downstairs
Nanna's fingers
brought shadow-butterflies to life along the wall.
Noon. The boy

in the comfort of fever, Nanna
fussing about him, the red light burning
on the Pilot wireless, the world beyond
with its wars and winnowings whistling
to come in;

the monastery bell, in the distance told
angelus; always he would remember it, the harmony, Nanna
knocking her breast, announcing it, *and the Word
was made flesh*, and he, heedlessly, answering, *and dwelt
amongst us.*

*

Dear John:
    I enclose a crisp new ten shilling note. Keep doing well at your studies.
We have got the electric now and all the shadows have vanished from the
house. I miss them. Bluebottles keep banging off the bulbs in a misery of
desire. The television set brings war and bad news in the door. But I heard
Count John McCormack singing at the Eucharistic Congress and then
there was Canon Sidney McKeown and he sang 'Queen of the Angels and
Queen of the May'. Sometimes the television's face is nothing but a snow-
storm and a loud, whingeing noise. They are advertising everything
imaginable that could be in the whole world. I always pray, John, you will
have a vocation. Turn your desires ever towards God, all else leaves us in a
misery. Pray for me. I always pray for you.
    Your own loving
                Nanna.

We stood, her fingers moving on the beads, her lips
busy as if by multiplying words she might find the one
word that matters; all this waiting, she said, her hand
holding firmly to mine. By the path's edge – a daughter,
dead too young; in the deep grass the wider, double-blanket

grave, duvet of marble-chips, a space
reserved, she said, and you
are named for him, she said
and for the other John, the one Christ loved, John
evangelist.

A soft wind siffling through the grasses, a butterfly –
its cardinals and ambers – like the blown heart
fluttering;
wild iris, fuchsia, a dark and light-green opulence – and once
a dragonfly, stationary as an angel

on the air, its
membrane-wings and emerald-sheen
needle-body threatening –
and I held to a black and old-wool coat
and knew the tremors of her sorrowing.

In a corner, the piled
detritus, dead-heads, twisted wire-frames, a slow
smouldering, unholy
incense. She sniffled, once, and turned; a magpie,
brooming like a witch from a hawthorn hedge, began

its manic cackling.
Opalescence, opulence,
carrion, fungus, carse,
headstone, excrescence, growth; the bleak
sideways leaning of her pleading.

*

Dear Nanna:
   We have just finished singing Compline and I am in my cell. I always
enjoy singing the *Salve Regina*, even though everything is in Latin. My
cassock is hanging on the back of the door like a huge shadow. It is night

now, though early. There is still light outside and it will be difficult to
sleep. I have night prayers to say yet. Then it will be Matins, out of dark-
ness into Christ's light. I feel sometimes like Nicodemus must have felt,
sneaking into the presence of holiness. I feel, too, that I am of the salt earth
of the island and speak with the salt accent of that earth. The altar tonight
was crowded with lilies. You would have relished it. I pray for you night
and day. Pray for me. I need your prayers.

    Your own
        John.

*

Till there was death's imminence, her room
suffused with the chill that longing knows
when there is no future. She
shifted in the bed although we knew
she was already in eternity, her eyes, wide open, saw

beyond us, the dead, their clay-damp presences
passing through us, shadows
of absent bodies only the blind could see,
blind-man's-buff, desire
become a fire burning on the fuel

of its own flesh.
I was startled at a sound
as of soft finger-tips against the window: a moth
hopeless to get out through a pane
dense as the whole universe.

*

In the Great Silence I walked
on the long corridor, seminarian hands
in seminarian sleeves, urging myself to prayer; moonlight
through the high windows, I was a shadow
reaching for shadows, a ghost

haunting the traces of old longing. Seminarian
body, late adolescent stirrings, Nicodemus creeping out
into the light of the world. The longing, I was told,
for love, is already
love.

65

Drinking the Spring

We set out before dawn, relishing the heady scent of earth
wet after rain; in morning light

the valley flushed with flowers, with yellows, purples, blues.
Noon. A dustscape. Thirst.

We stalled, by Sychar, Bir Ya'kub, knowing that
down too deep to reach was living water. The others

left for the village; he, and I, exhausted, sat. A hawk
grew out of a speck of sky and dropped

suddenly, nearby; you could hear the wreck of its pouncing,
imagine a beast heart

commanding, another tiny heart
pounding under the quickening shadow. He had an eye, too,

for a beautiful woman and stirred, as I did, when she
dropped her pail

down into the darkness. The world
undulant with dry-boned travellers. Down, into the heart

of waters. And then
he would not drink of it, speaking to her

of the thirst within him, for being, and people, and harvests,
his eyes

on her in overwhelming love, till the man I thought
I was coming to know –

in whom I invested
body, soul, imagination, words – was other, his language

other, his word
I am reverberating everywhere, like a scream echoing

through a gorge. Silence then. Drops of the precious water
fell from the pail unheeded onto earth. The searing sun. Cicadas.

And when she turned from him at last, flushed
with pleasure, and the hawk

lifted again in its ecstasy
of living, I understood something

about being born once more
out of water,

and out of blood.

In the Teeth of the Wolf

She woke suddenly out of nightmare,
   and sat up, rigid; eyes
wide on darkness she would have cried
   had she been able. She had been

falling again, inert as stone.
   Speechless, our clinging
pleaded with You, and You were darkness. Her eyes
   blank as pebbles, anguish etched in marble

on her pallid face. Lupus. Now she feared
   sleep, feared daylight and its endless
wakefulness, the way a stone
   can't sleep, nor a block of timber, nor a nail.

*

I remember how the breeze
   came softly from the sand-dunes, the marram grass
thin-fledged and yielding;
   the beach, where the waves had been at play,

was rilled in hardened
   sand-ripples; gulls
screamed, fighting for picnic-scraps; it should have been
   a perfect day, save

for Your long courtship of the woman, Your
   fierce
grip already on her blood, crushing her
   from within.

Wolves
   long absent from the timberlands of Ireland, prowled
slavering about her, all energies reduced
   to the vegetative

mere
    conservation of her living;
the sea beyond us blue with brilliants, a ship
    crossing the horizon on some high adventure;

I imagined deck-chairs, drinks
    in tall glasses, chatter,
the goods and truths that are all
    parts of the clutter of the soul;

nothing in this world
    can justify the all-embracing passion of Your love, Your
egotistical ravenings, her
    pain.

*

I see her now in her soft-shoe shuffling
    through the grey haze of the asylum;
in her small cell, the urinary smell, the degradation,
    the walls enclosing, *can you hear*, she said, *the ocean?*

The frayed blue dressing-gown, the fingers
    picking over locker things, grapes and tissues,
pain burning through her blood and that gentle mind
    tossing like a boat unmoored.

I put my arms about her, to reclaim her, but my arms held
    only a space she no longer occupied.
I prayed for healing; *if a man*, You said, *ask his father for bread*
    will he reach him down a stone?

*

On those last days I knew that You had won;
    there was no source to drink from
to give her back some small
    motive for living; I prayed now

You'd take her gently from the world,
    so reduced a frame
could not support such anguish;
    her silk-sheen eyes

watched beyond my being. That sad
      loved head, the hair
so thinned I could see
      small patches of skull. Ascetic. You

I hated, anger giving me strength
      to face the corridors, the wards and kitchen-sickly smells. This
the end of Your creation, to reduce
      Your creatures to a quivering meat?

                              *

She opened her eyes, there was a small light
      burning in them, she held my hand and said
John, I'm tired.
      One breath, quiet as a kiss, moment

of passage, the
      intersection of earth and heaven, and You
reached me a stone, and I refused
      belief in You, Creator. Bridegroom. Wolf.

The Gravity of Flesh

Grace
in all his being,
but a grace beyond

identifiable grace. Stood,
absorbed, on the shore,
waters of the lake

plashing at his feet: the day the hinges of the world
screamed, opening. Wonderful, and
menacing. The way everything is given and acceptable, then

other.
Listen. I insist
on details, on all interstices

admissible. What is left
is mystery, not un–
acceptable. The crowds

pushed after him, zealotry of the hurt, the angers, crush;
I speak, note,
history, its strict solidity, the nasty residue

suffering has left on men. Facts. All
verifiable. The stench
from old wounds; how you quickly glance away from the routed

eyes of the blind. What I remember most
is how the sunlight coloured the ochre lakeshore stones
a perfect gold, before the clamorous

petulant
splashed there. And how the gentling breezes
shadowed the folds of his robes.

*

Surgeon:
as if he had sliced into the bowels and
bored into the brain until he knew the secret

passageways of distress;
the human family, wanting and discontent,
no sooner healed and fed than discontent again,

and wanting.
They lay on grass amongst the bone-
white stones, the halt, and flawed, the salt-grey heavens

watchful; he, too,
grown silent before human degradation, needing, I knew, to be
elsewhere, to be

lone. I watched how their teeth
tore at the fish-skin, how black fingernails ripped
the barley-breads apart.

They left, the shore-side
littered with their rags, their plasters, sticks,
with crumbs and the sucked

bones of fish, and thought
themselves
masters of the dance.

*

Our lives are water. Waves. We left him
heavy with his burthens, and night
fell suddenly about us. For a time

moonlight sang on the surface of the lake
till winds blew, and the waves raged, and the boat
lay heavy in the waters, rain

casting her sluggish, the sails
flopping thickly against the mast;
labouring. Hours. And scared. He

came, ghosting on the waters, terr–
ifying us the more, absorbed
in his own thinking, the scarce light

shadowing the folds of his robe. Came
aboard. Sighed. And slept. And the storms
died. What the eye

sees, and what the mind knows that the eye has seen, may yet
seem forever doubtful. We nudged
shore;

I was more distant from him then
than ever I had been, this
stranger,

this
foreigner, this
grace.

Lazarus, and the Migration of Storks

Came what I have most dreaded, this
  entering the cave. Stone,
    rock, and dust, a deadening heat, some

merciful shade; our friend
  had achieved perfection, and was dead.
    While we stood, hesitant, a lizard

colour of stone, and as still, materialised out of stone,
  small, lithe body, capable
    of instant, untranslatable

speed, its shortest distance between fear and home
  anything but a straight line,
    but for now, like us, waiting. I was distracted,

willingly, from the spaces of our grief, when a stone-grey
  cloud shadowed the lizard-shape and its small enigma
    blushed the whole body a gentle blue.

Almost no breeze, but, when I looked again
  there was a petulant, white and grey-blue, lowering sky;
    he was standing, lizard-still, in juniper shade

and all I could think of was how
  the juniper berry dries your whole mouth up with bitterness.
    I admired

his stage-managing of the event, the delay, the halt
  anticipation, and then the women, how they were left to savour
    bitterness, so they would stand the more

exalted. My instinct
  was to flee – not to become
    witness for him, but I stayed,

enthralled again by the weathers of the heart.
  Came the high flight of migrating storks, their long necks reaching,
    their thin, determined bodies, the leisurely

flapping of wings – they were making their way
        through sloughs of cloud and thunder-darknesses
                together, individually apart, and silent –

and when I looked again it was his tears
        softened me, making it possible to accept
                impossibility, how history

in its dull inexorable passing
        would skitter a little to the side, destroying
                all the mathematical certainties.

Came the high, authoritative naming, and then
        it was more than the mere
                opening of the black mouth of the cave letting the word

resurrection!

out; the grind and thuck of the rock
        shifting, and the soft fabric of what is real
                ripped quietly and we heard

the hesitant slap of his feet on ground, until,
        unwrapped, he stood, his hands
                heavy with gifts too generous for us.

I felt
        sorry for him, who had to find
                new purposes, and he looked back once

with some nostalgia. Meanwhile
        something like courage
                was seeding itself in my flesh,

touching the certainty of birds, the indifferent
        ripening of fruit, something that was
                more than hope, a little way less than love, less

than joy. By then, the day
        had moved to evening; the juniper-shade had lengthened
                into dusk; sleep, and the emptiness of sleep

seemed welcoming, and he
　　turned, and I
　　　　turned, into impossible futures.

Carnival of the Animals

Someone played piano in a far room: scales
growing out of black earth, blossoming, and falling back.

*

From outside, a cock's
hilarious response, all his hens
busily indifferent to his brass ego, indifferent too
to the honed axe-blade, waiting in the dark outhouse.

*

Badger, noon-time, after his night
hours of raids and rhapsodies,
roadside lies in dust, the stench of his decay
ghosting already on leaf and mayflower.

*

Cat comes, secretly, to the lupin-beds
to dream, will leave
bruised warm spaces, cat-sweet, like dreams; and big
bucko the hare comes lolloping through the wild meadow
to chew on the salt new leaves of the rose-bush;

*

for a moment, attendant on what is beautiful, I forgot myself.
But someone called from a far room: *John! John!*
and I was back again, in sunlight, hearing pitched
ongoing vibration of the one word: God; with the discordant

*

note: man, the un-
merciful; and the old song we all sing: God
is. And we
are not.

The Aftertaste of Bitterness

The roof slopes steeply;
I am listening to Bach, the St John Passion: *I live,*
the pleasures of love enjoying, and thou
art dying. How the attic space
has grown luxurious with the music, oboe

d'amore, a thunder-storm, a dulcet
rending of the heart in sorrow; and I fill,
if only for a moment, with
transcendental energy. Clouds
through the skylight window shift, reform,

there falls a huge knocking on the glass
from the opened sky. Peter's
ham-fisted effort at violence, the swung
sword; then the music of healing, the forgiving
hand. *And what is truth?* I'm drawn away

by mating-shouts of pheasants
in the high grass outside. Bach's slow chorales
lift the soul, through time, out
beyond time, till the music tells how death
is the perfect state of innocence.

*

Truth is this: the weak
pitch themselves bodily against might; violence,
the swung
sword, comes with un-

anticipated speed, and dwells
in the slow absurdity of dream; this
is truth: jagged-edged girders shape a cross
that has taken root where stone

burned down to ash. Still
burning. It will be difficult
to look to the sky again with confidence. Under
temporary hoardings a down-and-almost-out

was playing the flute-music of affliction; where, it sang,
am I to go from here? Humanity, alone in the universe, has learned
how to hate. What are the uses
of poetry? And its responsibilities? Imagine

the smaller things: a kitsch glass paperweight
on a desk, a man's
fingers fidgeting with it; a tall
girl walking across a hallway for a glass of chilled

water; and how it took so long (split
seconds) to see what it was that was pitching itself
bodily against them: the
future, and its sudden lack, and how the glass

melted instantly, the fingers with it, how the water
scalded suddenly, the tall girl
with it; and countless other
instances: the stuff of gravity; and finally how the distance

between us and God is
death. I listened to the patient
whine of air-conditioning in my hotel room; a man
in Washington Square performed

the dream-like Tao dance; leaves on the trees
have shaken themselves free
of dust; streets are decked out again
in the decorum of commerce. Affliction

leaves an aftertaste of bitterness, like sloe-juice
cramping the tongue; and nowhere can you hear
the poem of *Father, forgive them*; it is might, seeking
to be mightier. I dressed

in my blue shirt, my priest-black
trousers, settled my papers to performance mode,
sought weighted words, to say to the hopeless *hope*
to the unforgiven *mercy*, my tongue

was swollen in my mouth, language
needing to start over. I set out
down the indifferent streets to where I must speak:
Sometimes, in impossible places...

Belovèd

I cry out, to wake myself from nightmare;
a man is stooping over another man
and driving nails in through the living flesh.

A soldier knows no distance between his violence
and the quivering of the dreadfilled soul;
I touched the rough timbers, where his feet were wracked,

my fingers came away, slicked with his blood,
I took my fingers to my lips and licked them clean,
tasting wine and salt. The whole body

spasming, the bone-web of the hands extended
into tearing, the chest heaving; he was labouring
to make the body essence. Blood in the white of his eyes

and spittle-blood dribbling on his breast, his head
too heavy and every possible bodily pain
clenching him. What terrified me most

was his consent, a subjugation, like
stork-flight, like lizards, like stone, as if
a reconciliation were to be effected.

I wanted to touch the bones visible, like light, under his flesh
and held instead the mother, while her hard hands
kneaded mine, and when at last he screamed out *it is over*

the angel of human circumspection flapped once his wings
abandoning the earth. There was a threshold of darkness
that the darkness crossed, disrupting ground, and I saw scorpions,

turd-brown, ecstatic, emerge into failing light.
A dead body weighs like stone, the spirit gone
that had held it up, like wings, like light, gravity

filling up the spaces where there had been grace.
I put my arms, too, about the body, clinging to him,
closing my eyes and clinging to him as if my clinging

could haul back life. That which we cannot bear, which will
come, affliction, leaves an aftertaste of bitterness
like juniper-berries cramping the mouth;

I rocked, a while, inert matter, and would will
all caesars nightmares of truth, would curl their tongues
once about the one word, love. There was birdsilence,

earthsilence, darkness. I kissed the stone mouth, my tongue
touching the stone lips, lover, belovèd, this
cave of darkness, this earth, belovèd

earth. Our lives
water. Oh my belovèd
Palestine. My belovèd.

Report from a Far Place

for Fred Marchant

Sometimes, in impossible places, it is the small
illimitable pieces of the earth that will seduce you
back into grace: yellow sorrel in the hidden fissures,
the wren, spunk-tailed and pirouetting on the wood-pile,

splinters in the hewn timber you will relish
as imperfections. An orchid grows through wild grasses
the way the poem swells and will say *me!* this
being the first day again of all the world. You will be

witness to what a life saves out of the assault,
to prayers the defeated have no breath left to speak,
you will know the old, uncomplicated words

lifting once more like light, like love, like hope –
and you will find, at last, how the world writes itself
differently from what you had expected.

The Light of Dawn

A scattering of almonds on the earth, my feet
bruised and punctured where I ran. Dawn light
sending ministers of shade and mist-shapes
amongst the boles of trees, branches and blossoms all
on song. I could not wait. Then had to

wait, such hope
being too much. I glanced in, and saw
light, and linens folded. Sparrows
chipped and snickered as they do; an olive-
green butterfly slow-clapped its wings, silently,

gorging on a fire-red buttercup. It was one
moment out of uncountable moments, everything
hanging, while we waited for the childish one, elder
of the swung sword, his big
hands, his quick decisions. And she

stood beside me, blanched and trembling;
those full breasts, her hair in the dawnlight
tinged blue, and I knew, despite all miracles, my flesh desires
undiminished. Waiting. Came the soft-
fawn body of the hoopoe, small

whoosh of wings, and set herself
dust-bathing, that even from where I stood I knew
her musty stench, attar of skunk, her preen gland
labouring. Leaf-shadow, fruit-swell, all that
half-light waiting, all that

promise, with its attendant dread, and the world
straining, as if in prayer. Belief, decision
of the will, what the eye, the ego, sees and knows
that it has seen, and then the retina closing over
on what has not, insisting, ever been?

*

Night we spent on the lake, fishing.
You can hear voices, clear and intimate, over quiet waters.

Midnight, and after, we ate the sticky
sweet-syrup flesh of dates, falling giddy in the night-

warmth, moved naked on the boat's deck, our feet
slapping out lake-rhythms, staccato, innocent, slow.

We lay then, knowing the rounding of the constellations,
stars like apple-blossoms floating down from the arbour-sky,

how good it is to circle towards conclusion
in the original state of innocence. They slept. Once, I knew

where I lay cupping my genitals in my hand, that moon
and stars, mast, companions were all I ever needed, that I was

young, and vigorous, and the world was my demesne.
We woke, to laughter, to the ponderous elegance

of a flight of pelicans, shorewards, over the water, woke
to an insistent voice calling over the surface of the lake.

*

He was crouched over a fire on the lake shore.
I approached, slowly, as we all did, this stranger, this
familiar. There were blackened stones
where old fires had been. He cooked,

his fingers fidgeting with the shore-
stones, shifting them, the clack-
thuck of stone on stone irritating me; I sat
at a little distance, refusing, morning light

coming in quickly over the lake. I ate, then,
my fingers pinched from the scalding flesh
and I licked them, tasting
bread, and lake, and a soft inebriation.

It is the Lord, I thought, watching him, the hurt
hands, the caring... and I needed pain then, not only
the fish-flesh charred, but mine, to shove my fist
in where the flames grew, so I would know, for certain

it was real. He watched me, and my sudden tears
turned me from him, from lake and boat and world
and he, lake, boat and world blurred suddenly into grey
and I knew one day I would fall blind. It was then he said

I would live forever. I sat, suffering a while
the animal fondling of my hand in his, watched
the gathering of fish-bones, the smarled ash, and his
slow disappearance among the shore-line trees.

Prayer

Bring me ashore where you are
    that I may still be with you, and at rest.

Your name on my lips, with thankfulness,
    my name on yours, with love.

That I may live in light and know no terror of the dark;
    but that I live in light.

When I achieve quiet, when I am in attendance,
    be present to me, as I will be to you.

That I may hear you, like a lover, whisper *yes* –
    but that you whisper *yes*.

Be close to my life, my loves, as lost son to mother,
    as lost mother to son.
        But be close.

Come to me on days of heat with the cool breathing
    of white wine, on cold
        with the graced inebriation of red.
            But that you come.

That you hold me in a kindly hand
    but that you hold me.

Do not resent me when I fail
    and I fail, and I fail, and I fail.

That I may find the words.

That the words I find to name you
    may approach the condition of song.

That I may always love with the intensity of flowers
    but that I love,
        but that I always love.

V An Exemplary Fiction

The Red Gate

Mornings, when you swing open the red gate –
admitting the world again with its creeds and wars –
the hinges sing their three sharp notes of protest;
you hear the poplars in their murmurings and sifflings
while the labouring high caravans of the rain
pass slowly by; it will seem as if the old
certainties of the moon and stars, mingled
with the turnings and returnings of your dreams, mist
to unreality, although there rise about you
matins and lauds of the meadow-sweet and rowan; the first
truck goes ruttling down the wet road and the raw
arguments, the self-betrayed economies of governments
assault you so you may miss the clear-souled drops
on the topmost bar that would whisper you peace.

Mushrooms

A long, deep-rutted lane
        under elms. A cart,
its boards and shafts
        a fading red, a flaking
blue, bumpeting towards the tarred

road, the dunt, the lovely
        racketing of milk-churns
hoisted and deposited. Morning
        blessing itself into day.
And the cart returning, lightened,

to the farm-house, the lime-
        wash, the sheltering
sycamores. To the gathering
        of mushrooms in a far field,
their glistening under dew

and how they fistled soon
        on the stove-top, salt
bubbling to a brown juice
        and hissing
on the heat. To the aunt

wrapped in her daisied
        apron, her care fussing
through the stone-washed kitchen,
        as if love must always last,
apart, inside bird-song and rosaries

and the steady
        filling of the water-butt
under old eaves.
        There is a child forever
hesitant at the door – to be

called inside, the offering
        of a roasted mushroom, its
succulence, its yielding, the savour
        of the grazing of horses, of the
in-leaning passion of rains,

of the dank unleavened
      fecundity of clay, and the old
woman exultant in the giving,
      and the sweet and blood-shadowed
figure on the wall

explaining everything.
      The man (big by the mantelpiece,
hands tweaking the braces
      over an off-white vest – who will soon
manhandle you into laughter,

his chores stretching before him
      like rank outhouses of the first
days) will tell, evening,
      to the bass music of turf
fire, storms in the sycamores,

how they left
      the violated bodies to decay
in distorted shapes scattered
      on distorted fields, how his heart
failed him as he rescued the dead

in the black hiatus of night,
      made graves shallow
as the hollows between ridges,
      saw souls exhale
in phosphorescent iris-flowers

up through the deepest
      darkness he had ever known,
till she shooed him – to be telling
      nightmare tales to an
impressionable child (the dark

moth-soft in the lamplight) but I
      under wistful eyes of the God
showing his thorn-fenced heart, dreamt
      only of churns, of cart-horses,
of the spittling of juice on the stove.

The Big Men

Abraham

And then a consciousness may flicker
of the histories of suffering, of thin
patinas of glory set

immeasurably behind you, of bearded patriarchs,
their urgent prayers over the barren wombs of their women –
as you remember the beaten track up from Dookinella

over the shoulder of Mweelin, and down
to Dooega graveyard; big men – lowering the coffin
so they and the dead might rest together – took stones

from their pockets to signal
holy ground, the hard heart of the country. Beyond all that
the high and necessary God, the violent, whose judgements

are suspect and whose edicts
hearten the sly, the bullying, whose punishments
issue suddenly, are heavy-handed, and serene: something to do

with the studied, mathematical necessities. We coloured in
Bible history pictures, red
for the slaughtering sea, for the bush on fire, for the blood

of Samson's depredations; and for the father's heart, that agèd man
who drew his child up the mountainside, prepared, unacceptably,
to slit his throat. The schoolroom, small and dim, was coloured

dismal brown; we were learning God, whom we coloured
dismal brown, his beard
doughty with authority; like those big men in the album,

upright in black, on their high-strung motors, their small
wives holding grimly on their arms; or great
grandfather, certain of his ground, his body

thick with the nineteenth century, till a small boy's heart
misgave him, though he went on suffering
exemplary fictions, old warriors, the sepia photographs.

The Mother

Rebekah

We are close still to the beginning.

The woman sits, abstracted, on volcanic rocks, (we
hold our breathing, to watch: she has gone past
the fleeting moment of youthful and womanly
perfection) her knees drawn up, her eyes

watching out over the ocean, the breezes
touching her flesh, the way for centuries they have sifted
minutest dust along the basalt crevices, treasuring
the roots of thrift, sea-holly, campion.

She has loved. The beauty of the man. And his response,

how, together, they had sensed at last some order.
She is still, now, though one black curl
tassels to an unseen touch; the body,
content a while, will be torn from within, there has been

upset already, dissension, an all-pervading fear
shivering her flesh – is this, she thinks,
answer to prayers? is this the to-be
mother's

lot? Two

nations in permanent contention, those deprived
blowing themselves apart in strategic cities,
those sealed in power
trampling down the earth with cruel nonchalance;

and her two big sons, in rivalry,
shall they return, contrite, to her knees?
It is terrible
to be a woman, to be loved

is terrible, and terrible to give birth, terrible to fear

love, to split apart, like un-
regenerable stone. We are close still
to the beginning, close
to sorrow, to the vast and ever-

expanding sea-scape of unknowing.

Husbandry

Eyes watching out of another picture. Another
life. Familiar, and unknown. Younghusband. Gauche.

Skinproud, slimtall, father. There is a long
back garden, a terraced house, small windows

open; shrubberies, hydrangeas maybe, but it is he
the focus of our attention, and of his: the hands

stumped in trouser pockets, hefting the buttoned jacket
awkwardly; casual-alert, it is the stack of hair

surprises, with that confident self-gratulatory grin
supporting a cigarette, as if he has grown master

of all the secrets of husbandry, or as if
he would stride out of the past with all

the answers. Dead now. Departed. Old
faithful. Cherished. Belovèd. Nor ever understood.

The Poem

Jacob

Like waking out of dream
imagining you have been listening to the mice
busy among the papers
or to ghost-footsteps up and down a stretched ladder

and now, in the darkness, nothing
because your eyes are open on the darkness
that will not yield to your insistence
until you yield to it.

Spaces of Peace

Mary Jo Connors

She is here, alone, caught (as the poem catches) in black
and white, in cheerfulness – a café near Pompeii,
a pause in the cruising, 1938; they are sitting

at a small ironwork table, placed and posited
for the camera; long skirts, long smiles; she
raising her glass with the best of them

happy in youth and in the joys
of journeying; carafes, straw bowlers and somewhere,
out of picture, U-boats in preparation

and heavy-booted men in their march-past
towards the future. Cheers! Here's to the son
as yet undreamt of, here's to the poem

still sixty-and-several years away, here's to the soul
daring its flight towards happiness and love.
When Jacob looks up and sees Rachel, her assured

approach, the radiance of youth about her, the riotous
dance of death will already have begun. The way
bullets dance up dust along the earth, the way

the upward-swinging arms of the explosion
shape out a singular elegance. We imagine
spaces of peace, gardens where love, like lilies,

grow for a time in God's care, but we know
wars do not end, they hesitate awhile, like stanzas,
and take up again, more fiercely.

Brothers

We are close to the start of sorrow.
Brothers born; and twins. Of two brothers
one is of water, and one
of sky. The need for order. The love of dis-
order. The natural music
of Abraham and Isaac and Esau

become cacophony: Abraham, Isaac, Jacob.
I was high in the branches of a pine-tree
the day he came: uncle; out of that
North African photograph, 1942,
six perfect young men lined up and smiling, feet
apart, hands behind backs, the pilot's caps

carefully askew. Behind, and above them,
the black barrelling engine, the two-man-wide
and elegant propeller, the lethal wings –
Spitfire, and men-at-war. I feared him
who had doled out death
and had fallen out of skies with unnatural noise;

sophisticate of slaughtering, with hidden
never-to-be-healed
memories, reaching, perpetually for oblivion.
The other: sailor, and lover. I was
standing on the quay at Westport, by the insistent
peaked summit of the sacred mountain – under subtle

xylophone pluck-music of rigging and soft rainfall
on the water – when he came from the pub, a big
glass of Lucozade in his fist for me – and put
a two-shilling piece into my hand, and asked me
for patience; high-seas man, farer and wanderer – see him
in the album, ageing, light-blue suit a burden, shirt

and tic, triangle of kerchief in top pocket, and floweret
in the buttonhole – attending again for marriage, bemused
self-mocking man, contrite and falling, eager only
for understanding, and the all-quelling lights-out of drink.
Brothers. We are all so slight of soul we crave
mercy, deeming that God may be taken in

by our political posturings. These are the dark
origins, mythic and unsure, morass on which we walk,
where luscious orchids grow. Bury one by water,
who is laid to rest on a stilled ocean; and the other,
wracked and wearied, laid on upbearing air
where mornings rise for him, at last, unmenacing.

Age of Foolishness

In February winds, bunting round the chapel
created desultory applause; in the grey house opposite,

with its smell of contained turf-smoke, of lingering
mutton-fat and stews, the old woman sat, listening;

only the finger-ends had vision now, though the years
had roughened them, her eyes like the mucous-blob

of the oyster-flesh, as she touched and probed, to light
her cigarette from the frightening stove mouth. Her blindness

filled her with salutary figments while I read to her
The Song of Hiawatha or a chapter out of Genesis.

The first death: never to see the stars again
in perfect stillness on a perfect night. Her hard hand

touched my hair, as if I were a favoured son, offering
blessing. Sometimes she stood in the chill air

expecting the ordered flight of geese, though they flew
at an unconscionable height; then at night she prayed,

a gathering of slumped flesh in a wicker chair, in a dark
within darkness. The second death: so many ways

out of the world, and each impossible. Impossible, too,
the patience, the trust, the unquestioned fictions.

Blessing

May your heart melt, for ruth,
for pity of your brothers – let them not
bow down before you, that God may give you
abundance of light in an age of darkness;

may the angel touch your lips, though gently,
with the red-hot coals of verbs;
that the wild meadow of your living
be rife with orchid, butterbur and clover;

that the great ocean that is time
offer you plentiful catches of mercy, and the tides
washing on your defences be cleansing merely;
that you consent to the growth of trees and know

the ecstasy of attention to each pouting leaf –
that your days be fluid as the melodies of birds
and may each note of your evensong
build to the lift and lift of Gregorian chant;

may you know you are nothing and may that nothing
become in you the wholeness of eternity;
may your growth be strong as holly,
and may the lie of violence

never sound against your ears; and when,
at death's astonishing moment, you come to know
the pity that is in the truth, may you have attained
at last, the fluency of water.

Patricia's Story

and Jacob's dream

Imagine a stretch of barren land, something like earth
in the beginning, before man's
curious incursions and violations, but imagine it

nothing like this Bunnacurry graveyard
that was kempt when the young woman died;
there was a path then,

shore-sand trodden hard, clay mounds with names and dates
written in shells, pretty-
patterned, white sea-stones at head and feet and white

sea-stones shaping a cross.
Dreamlike.
Nothing like that. Forget all that. Think, perhaps,

of the ocean, without the blossoming
of waves or the jollying over the surface of sleek sea-flesh;
the beautiful young woman's name

was carved into lichened stone. Start
again. Start
tabula rasa.

Extent of scrub and desert-land, erratics, nude earth, no
trees; emptiness under a grit-hard sky;
aspiration to beauty being the force that tenses us, she

was beautiful, the fiction says,
and true. Each fiction linked into another, the long
chaplet of history

rounding towards its source. Admit her, then,
insistent on the landscape; the graveyard gate is painted iron
and does not squeal

on opening while all around the woman's grave
are flowers, glass
panniers of tears, death-cards; here is the house of God, here

the gate of heaven. Start
again. He has moved a little on the journey, and is tired,
no shelter anywhere and night

however lovely, with stars and silence, will fall
chill; there will be
scorpions and creeping things and the head of a man asleep

will need support. Stone
angels in the graveyard, their eyes blanks, their whorled wings
folded, will keep

perfect guard, knowing their place, knowing too
how she died, how disease was a shroud
over the land and how the land cried out, in silence,

for a more desirable future. Sea
in the distance, the sound like the whispering indifference
of God – and the lush

loveliness of bramble-bush and whitethorn,
the busy
coin-counting calling of wrens, erratic

purposiveness of butterflies and the slow shifting of soil
over decomposing bodies. The man –
with stone for pillow – entering at last

the nightmare of faith,
angels crowding the rungs of the ladder, the God
slouching self-consciously against the sky.

What is the weight
of an angel? Do the ladder's rungs
sustain their feet,

and do they ferry souls into the heavens
out of grimness, or down out of light into the fluent
womb? Patricia's story,

the eschatology of an exemplary woman. Here
the house of God, the gate of heaven.
And when, the story says, he leaves at last, this suddenly

wiser man, closing
an imaginary gate behind him on an acreage
of emptiness, he will leave

the precious stone of his imagining
upright on the earth, as a memorial inscribed, a pitching-post
for ownership and inevitable violence.

Spaces before War

Jacob's Well

In barren places, even among crowds, the traveller
sits solitary; because these are still
beginnings there is little he can gather about himself

(she)(herself) for comfort; but there is vigour in being
young, lost almost, stopping by chance (by chance?)
in a beautiful place (and every place is,

in itself, beautiful) (difficult, near the beginning, to find
form); there are sheep, off-white
from the rubbings of sky and trailings of clay,

their lush indifference (and fear) cropping (like us) wherever
nourishment is to be found, their teeth, busy
in small mash-sounds, rippings of grass,

while they shift (like us) absorbed, across the earth.
And the man sits lazing in the sunshine,
flicks stones across the slope, imagining, the shaped

structure of the well behind him, the waiting
song of the water (the yielding. And she, later, lifting
wine in the glass, and gazing into it, its clarity, its cloudiness,

sits, imagining too, the waiting, the man), the yielding.
There is a space before every war for such
imaginings, for the easing of flesh and spirit towards some

meaningful commitment, small
energies conveying sustenance, where the soul
gathers itself (towards poetry) towards harmony, towards love.

The Marriage Settlement

Snowdrops are lifting out of the brown drench
of winter; here, in a neat and childish hand,

on the devoted page of the Family Bible, is written
the marriage date: first of June, nineteen hundred

and forty. War, of course, churning the earth sour.
Above the names, androgynous angels hover

in plum-coloured draperies and bearing wreathes. But
in the big album from the sideboard drawer, there is

no picture of them together, no bridal dress,
no formal suit – as if this ministering to love

is not to be recorded. They settled to a certain
Catholic dimness, to the deep indigo colouring

of shame, to kitchens, children, work, the long
necessary managing of days. Until the ultimate,

near-childish tears when death hove between them,
leaving the bulk of cut and milk-white lilies

withering on the turned earth.

On Land and Sea

Up here the cliff-grass strains out of clay
and sand; the mountains lean away, across
dulled and barren backlands; so much behind us

of the grit and liquid of our living;
my attention to you bids me always
strain with longing, our great fragility

floating on our strength, our strength dependent
on fragility. I would have laboured
seven years to win you, then seven more and they

have been as days, because you fence me round
with bliss. The ripping of old ivy
off the holly bark, how it comes away

with a disgruntled sigh, though blood-red berries now
will rise the higher. In the black, wind-filled
spaces of the night, when the trees seem driven

like innocents, apart, I cling to you
and moan our passing, out of these riven fields,
towards ocean; in the roiling waters

though you are pier and harbour, I would we two
could be coracles together, so equally
conforming to the lift and fall that

in this lift and fall we will find complete
stillness, beyond landfall, beyond
the breakers. Attending still. Though

broken. Be silent foam-flight with me from the rough
waves' crests, like flights of minuscule
white birds shoreward, that after long passage

come to rest awhile at the wild cliff's base.

The Dromedary Caravans

i.m. Tony O'Malley

Morning, and the red gate
    opening; on the roadway wind–
patterns of hailstones in dawnlight,
    tracks of a car-wheel over packed
mud. The blackthorns, stark and
    leafless, rose chilled and wet

while a solitary blackbird
    called. House to gate, astonishing
lichens making a green blush
    through tarmac; every journey taken
is a journey towards home.
    I set out as that day's light

thickened grey, with a slanting
    rain visible against the street-lamps' glow;
only the crossing of the orange fox
    hoisted the possibility of miracle
to the day. Day
    for the laying into rest of the man

who had found, at last, his way
    into the uncoloured, still point
at the soul of his paintings; lay,
    prepared for the journey, in favourite
floppy hat, best shoes, one box
    of charcoal pencils, the instruments

of his art, against his breast. I thought
    of an old woman scattering leaves
from the tea-pot to the stone floor
    so the dust might lie while she was sweeping:
shush, little one, was the whispering,
    shush, and shush, and shush; a journey

taken. Afternoon, rooks were insolent
    on the road where a grain truck spilled
unwitting plenty and, near home, the shattered
    body of a fox, it is difficult
to look on any passing
    with a measure of indifference.

Still not far from the beginnings
    the dromedary caravan moves on, lengthening
shadows across ridgeway sand;
    as if humanity and all that it contains
were labouring under the impulse
    of uncontainable desire; journeying,

somewhere, home. Remember Jacob –
    his farmyard of wives and sons
and concubines – calculating, chosen;
    chilled nights, the steel insistence
of the stars, the howled resentment of animals
    disturbed. The river, holding. With war

lust pricking in his veins. The angels
    consorting with him, and the God
(unacceptably) prospering his loins,
    his ego. Home, it may be, home
is not the journey's end: God is, perhaps
    only in the journeying

By the River

Days, with their breathless beauty, pass us by
like slurred words strung out in sentences. We know
there is a halt to every journey; this

side of the river, no obligation yet
to cross. Alone. Night fallen. Stars
brilliant in the stillness.

By day you can see them, the black water-drops
from an overhanging bank; you can hear
the swirl-pools of the water, the silken

swavering of long green weeds into the flow. By night
the world is suffering its beauty, bridled, like the stars, the taste
of our mortality being bitterness.

A step on the hard ground, a figure
shaping out of the darkness.
But there is no hard ground. Mud

flats, where the river curves, broadening. Strange-billed birds
scoop and stab in the glaur and shift
in sudden slaughtering; where no human foot finds

purchase, depths and their stench unthinkable. Footsteps
as if the photo-album had released its dead
with their burdens of loss and humours, bringing us

the need to stand believing, a knowledge of how
the body becomes soul, so we wrestle through the night
with the concept of consent, so we

agree, at last, to step up and yield
to those who crucify, those who mock the flight
of the wild duck, who skulk in reedy places and shoot

the lovely bodies down in mud.
Warriors. Whose firmest statement will be
violence, indifference, death.

An all-night concentration of desire,
until we name the invisible *desirable*, and name it
good.

God.
Peace. Till death
roots in our bones and we walk henceforth

limping, victorious. The shell-duck lifting on the dawn, calling,
this side of the river. No obligation yet
to cross.

The Chaplet

I can go back, quiet as a ghost, from here
where sweet coals whisper in the grate, I can go back –
while hailstones sputter against the panes outside – to see her
standing in the doorway, snow falling softly, an old woman's
spotted apron holding her, and know that she
is watching too, ghosting inwards and going back, visiting
her losses, as if she could find a way
to string it all together, to a sentence, making
sense, and I can sit remembering –
and shaping, the way a sonnet shapes –
that dusk her rosary burst asunder and beads
spilled skittering all-which-ways on the stone floor
as if her prayers and aspirations left
nothing in her shaking hands but a thread, bereft.

VI Seasons in Hell

Holy Saturday

I woke early. That old oppression in the gut.
Lifting out of nothing, into day, and its demands.
After the excess of Friday this is nowhere, the God
waiting out his days in loneliness, as we wait,
weathering. It is spring; magnolia blossoms
are streaked already with decay. The artist in his youth
was a dawn chorus, finding the green God voluble; now this
is the day, the Son dead, the Father is inaccessible.
Ivy, the painter said, favours the older oak, and sadness
favours the man; art comes to be a question of the body's will,
the mind's fore-warning. Outside, the hydrangea bush
is a skeleton of twigs, crossed everyway, with brown
mop-heads where the flush has been. We pray
that human beings will hold each other against the storms.

The Artist in his Youth

Open, O Lord, my lips, here where a drumlin of furze
is a Provence of broom; allow us the instruments of redemption:
easel, canvas, pen. While I sing praise
for cherry-trees in bloom, for a peach branch in blossom.
In the darkness behind morning I have left
nightmare : the outhouse, the rat in a dim corner,
busying itself through turf-mould; there are gnawed bones,
and sharp eyes focusing in hatred. But, this dawn,
the portals of suffering have been re-opened, this death
a form of birthing, and birth
a measuring into death. Father had set a pint glass
with bluebells and clear water on the window-ledge;
my tongue will announce your praise
and the full palette of the world speak psalmody.

Boot-Prints in Snow

Saturday; an old man in a farmyard, burdened,
a child, seated in grass, absorbed in a daisy-chain;
soon to find the God of righteousness and grief,
of mine-shafts and hovels, something
of a disappointment. I found myself – once, then often –
in tears before the artist's life, his almond boughs in bloom
between blue sky and melting snow, who knew Christ
an artist greater than all others, scorning clay and paint
to work on the living flesh. Vincent, who found sorrow
a seed implanted. On the botched canvas of the world
coal-miners, trudging home, left
tick-tock botched boot-prints on the face of snow,
processions of orphan men like rows of pollard
willows. Saturday today, the Christ-man dead.

Terre Cuite

I crept, for shelter, under a cowshed overhang,
rain falling through a grey light; I was startled
by the wrenching yawp of a donkey
complaining of the world's weight. I stood, washed
by light glinting off the bars of a gate, one high-gloss
impossible dragonfly hovering in the ditch. The draggled
drain-fed irises were yellow lamps and I prayed to God
for lumpen man who walks in lumpen boots
on commonplace ground; can you grow a canvas skin
and colour the bitter earth to acceptable bitterness?
bistre, terre cuite, mud, and withering grass.
In the near distance the ambivalent thud
of an ash-bucket; that difficult man
burning with a wild fire that nobody came to cherish.

Hero

That day the blackthorn in the wild-row hedge
exuded an Easter radiance; the last snowdrops
in by the shade stood like youths in short-sleeved shirts
peering out towards light. That the Christ
dropped out of day into tombed darkness, the
second death, the God-abandonment, is scandal;
like the artist, who painted the tempest
in the veins of sunflowers, another such
vulnerable hero who went down into the abyss of himself
and came back, painting peach-blossom radiance
and hoarding sunlight in golden coins
against familiar dark. Like stars as multitudinous
as the stars on the blackest night, the blackthorn,
its sour-milk blossoms against black boughs.

Foxgloves

Noon, and visiting hour. How the soul shrank
away... Arched corridors, doors off, and that pervasive
human-towards-healing smell. That day she smiled, some
small lift back towards light. I placed the foxgloves –
lilac-coloured, spotted dark like erotic nightmares –
in a tumbler on the window-ledge. This was somewhere
God could not go, this inbetween and nowhere, this life
in solidarity with the dead. Hell is no place,
unreleased demons floundering in their ego-cells;
poor fighter, and poor, poor sufferer. I would make all men
pleasing unto God, for the sake of mercy. I prayed:
make of my heart of flesh a heart of stone.
She set the foxgloves straight inside the glass. Watched
out through the barred window towards apple-trees in bloom.

Redemption

I sit, at evening, by the patio window; beyond
clusters of white rowan-blossoms are whispering
against silence. I wonder at my compulsion: can this word-
framing save me? or bring redemption to the half-made God?
And how does He interpret it? Self-portraits?
With Spirit: with Son and bandaged flesh?
Vincent thought poetry more terrible, painting
more dirty and I have wept for him, useful
for nothing, this hangdog nomad of the canvases;
believe, if you can, that a poem is a reasonable thing.
Can art redeem us? A vase of purple iris against a yellow
background, can it affect our shameful
politics, our aggrieved lusts? This darkest evening
of our unknowing, rooks gathering, the lilacs beaten down.

Daffodils

See the man! Standing on Scheveningen beach, sand
whistling round his ears as he paints, red hair burning
with fire raging from beyond the heavens;
madman, lover, willing to give away
the kingdom of his heart; became a scandal to us, painting
infinity, how the bearded iris grows
to a man's height. He would live like a monk
and visit the brothel every second week; in the dark night paint
an impossible star. In a still farmyard
the fire grew too hot and when he died, they set an easel,
folding-stool and brushes by the coffin; such
a short life, crowded with suffering; that by his poverty
we might grow rich; he died, and behold! he lives forevermore.
I drop, now, these small bouquets over his grave.